NATIONAL GEOGRAPHIC KiDS

CREEPY CRAWLY

STICKER ACTIVITY BOOK

Pull out the sticker sheets and keep
them by you as you complete each page.
There are also lots of extra stickers to
use in this book or anywhere you want!
Have fun!

NATIONAL GEOGRAPHIC
Washington, D.C.

Consultant: Richard Walker
Editorial, Design, and Production by
make believe ideas

Picture credits: All images Shutterstock unless noted as follows:
Dreamstime: 10 bl ant with yellow leaf, 18–19 background,
20 tr spiny orb weaver, 23 tr, 32 tl; tr, 36 tr, 37 ml bearded dragon,
Jurgen Otto: 19 m peacock spider, **Make Believe Ideas:** 1 tm ants,
10 bl black ant; bl; br ant trio, 11 tm; tr; mr ants,
16 m centipede, 17 mr centipede, 40 bl ants.

Sticker pages: All images Shutterstock unless noted as follows:
Dreamstime: 2, 3 red ant, 10, 11 large ant; ant with yellow leaf, Extra Stickers
(sheet 2) green beetle, 22, 23 scorpion in frame, 32, 33 harlequin poison dart frog;
red-headed poison dart frog, 36, 37 bearded dragon, **Make Believe Ideas:** 10, 11 black ant;
ant with blue leaf, 12, 13 green beetle, 16, 17 beetle, 22, 23 small scorpions, 24, 25 snail,
26, 27 fire truck; car, 30, 31 mice, 34, 35 beetle; fly, 36, 37 yellow butterfly,
38, 39 blue butterfly, 40 green beetle, Extra stickers (sheet 8) red snake,
Matt Propert/NGS: 30, 31 rattlesnake,
Jak Wonderly/NGS: 32, 33 golden mantilla frog.

Printed in China. 18/MBI/3

Lots of creatures creep and crawl.

All insects have six legs and a body made of three parts.

Dwarf epauletted fruit bat

rose chafer

Use the key to color the beetle.

1. green 2. red 3. orange

Weighing in at a very heavy 550 lbs (227 kg), the green anaconda is the largest snake in the world!

Help the bee through the maze to find its nest.

Start

Finish

Watch out for the bee roadblocks!

Honeybees live in groups with thousands of other bees!

3

Insects come in lots of shapes!

Bees, ants, butterflies, and wasps are all types of insect!

mint-leaf beetle

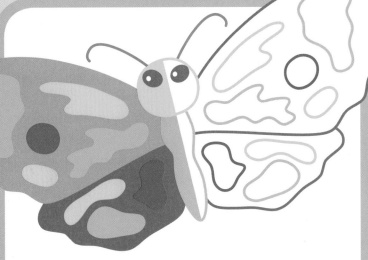

Color the other half of the butterfly.

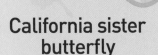
California sister butterfly

Find all five words to finish the word search.

ant
antenna
bee
body
wasp

h	a	b	p	a	w
r	n	t	o	o	a
w	t	r	x	d	c
a	e	o	a	r	y
e	n	o	n	b	b
g	n	t	f	e	a
w	a	s	p	e	a

yellow jacket

comet caterpillar

The comet moth caterpillar turns into a beautiful, giant moth. The moth's ribbon tail can grow longer than your hand!

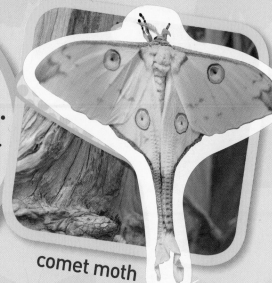
comet moth

Sticker praying mantises in the garden.

The praying mantis is great at spotting prey. It can turn its head all the way around to look behind itself!

5

Bees can have **venomous** stings.

Bees can smell, touch, taste, and hear through their long antennae.

hairy-footed flower bee

honeybee

ivy bee

small garden bumblebee

shrill carder bee

red clover

aster

ivy

foxglove

Find the missing stickers, then follow the lines to find out which flower each type of bee likes best.

bee

Bees have fuzzy bodies, but wasps are smooth.

wasp

Color the nest, then count the bees!

_____ How many bees?

7

Dragonflies are expert fliers.

Dragonflies fly with curled legs to make a basket shape. They use this basket to catch insects!

Dragonflies can fly backward and hover in one spot!

Use the key to color the dragonfly.
1. purple   2. blue   3. pink   4. green

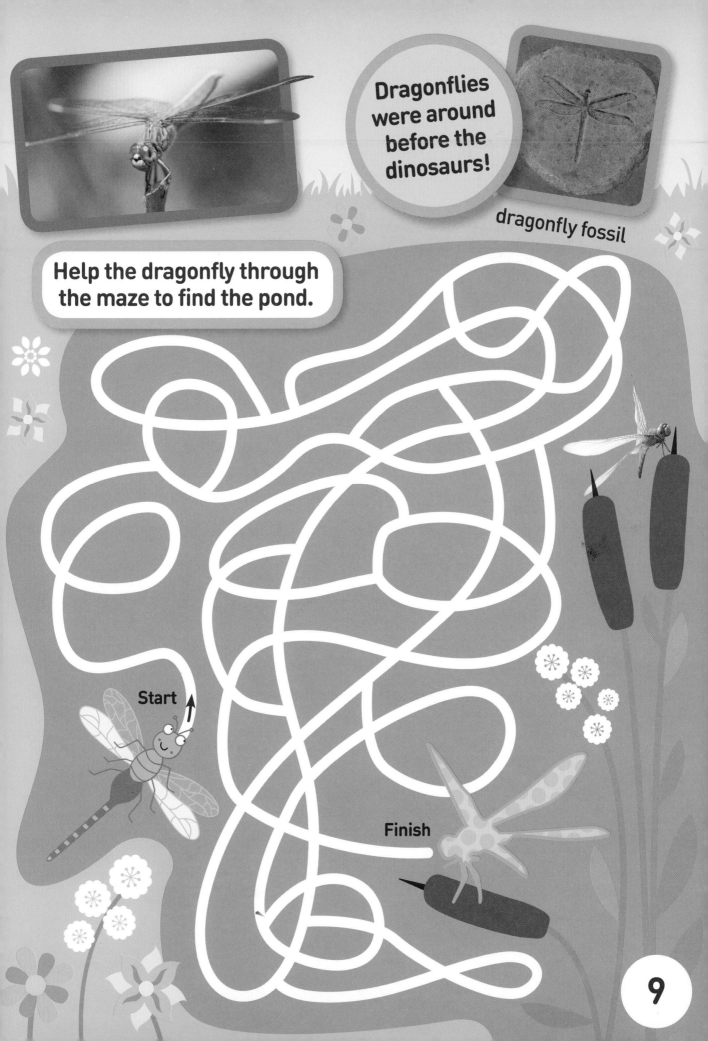

Dragonflies were around before the dinosaurs!

dragonfly fossil

Help the dragonfly through the maze to find the pond.

Start

Finish

Many ants work together!

leaf-cutter ants

Ants have different jobs to do. They work together to move and collect food, and also to attack!

leaf-cutter ant

wood ant

fire ants

Find the missing stickers to finish the patterns.

Leaf-cutter ants carry leaves back to the nest for food.

Many ants, like wood ants, build underground nests with long tunnels. Draw and color your own tunnels to finish the ant nest!

The bulldog ant is the most dangerous ant in the world! It bites its victim with its mouth and stings with its tail!

bulldog ant

There are about 8 million types of **beetles!**

Dung beetles roll dung into balls, then push the balls away and bury them until they are ready to eat.

Find the ball of dung that's different.

black-headed cardinal beetle

Asian long-horned beetle

Sticker mint-leaf beetles eating the leaf.

giraffe weevil

12

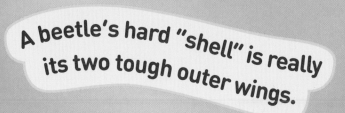

A beetle's hard "shell" is really its two tough outer wings.

The world's fastest beetle is the Australian tiger beetle. It can run up to 5.5 mph (9 km/h).

Give the beetle colorful wings.

Do you have **beetles** in your backyard?

Farmers love ladybugs because many of them eat the tiny insects, called aphids, that destroy crops.

Use the key to color the picture.

1. purple   2. red   3. green   4. black

Sticker the ladybugs.

Ladybugs come in lots of colors!

firefly

Most fireflies can make light with their bodies. These fireflies come out at night.

Find the missing stickers, then count how many fireflies are in each jar and write the answers.

Millipedes and centipedes have lots of legs!

A centipede has one pair of legs for every segment of its body, while a millipede has two pairs.

Find the millipede sticker.

centipede

millipede

Color the centipede.

Millipedes have lived on Earth for over 400 million years!

Find the missing stickers, then draw lines to match the clues to the correct millipede.

This millipede has bright yellow stripes.

This millipede is shiny and black.

yellow-banded millipede

pill millipede

pink dragon millipede

Spiders have eight legs.

Some spiders spin webs, others live in burrows, and some even use their silk like a balloon to fly over huge distances!

Chilean rose tarantula

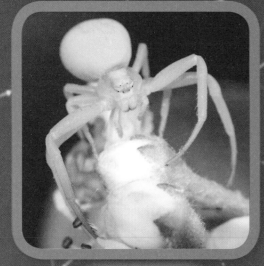
crab spider

 Sticker insects in the spider's web.

zebra spider

Banana spiders are also called golden silk spiders because of their yellow silk!

banana spider

Peacock spiders have colorful patterns.

Mexican red-kneed tarantula

Design a pattern for the peacock spider.

Some spiders are unusual shapes!

Spiny orb weavers look dangerous, but they are actually harmless! Their spikes warn birds not to eat them!

The bird-dung spider looks like bird poop!

Find all five words to finish the word search.

legs

web

spider

spike

venom

s	p	i	k	e	s
u	a	t	o	w	p
w	u	b	x	v	i
l	e	g	s	e	d
e	a	w	e	n	e
g	n	e	l	o	r
s	e	b	s	m	a

jumping spider

Arizona blond tarantula

Stickers for pages 2 and 3

Stickers for pages 4 and 5

Extra stickers

Stickers for pages 6 and 7

Stickers for pages 8 and 9

Extra stickers

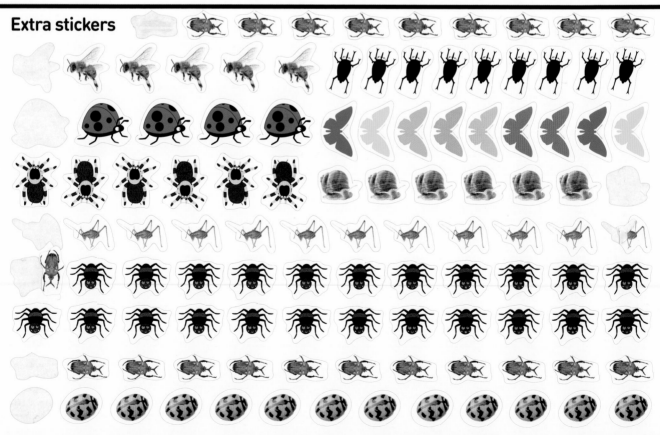

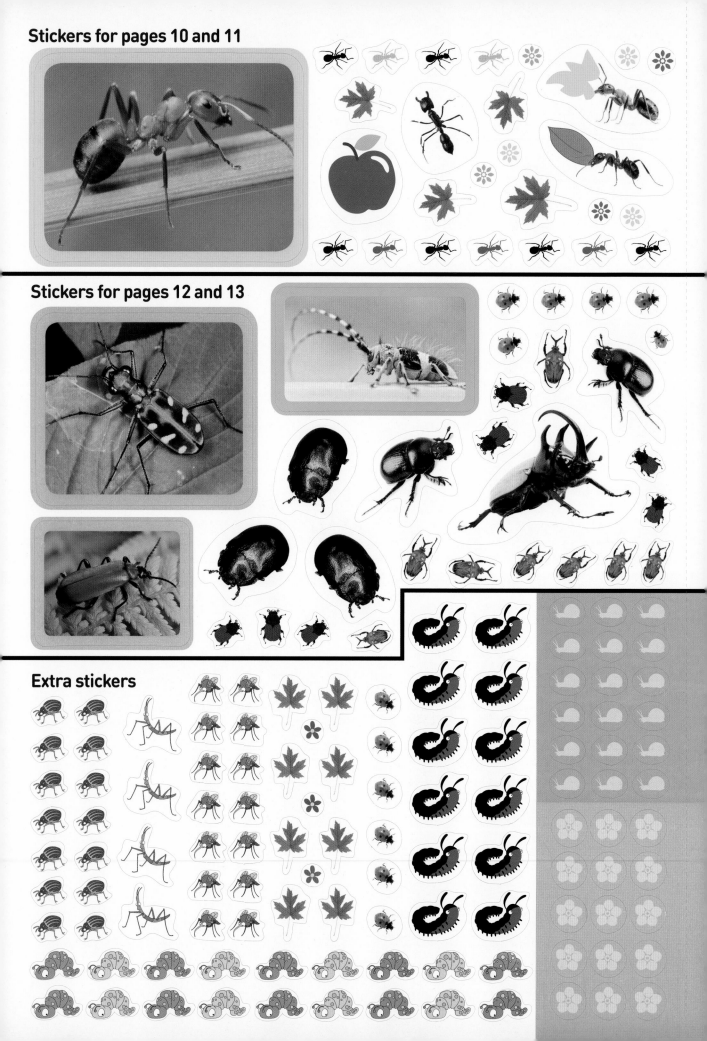

Stickers for pages 10 and 11

Stickers for pages 12 and 13

Extra stickers

Stickers for pages 14 and 15

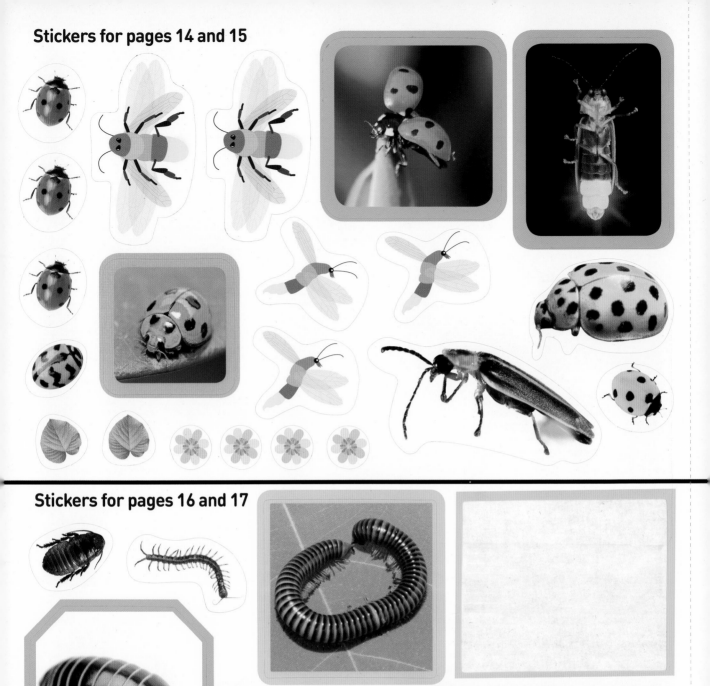

Stickers for pages 16 and 17

This millipede is bright pink and has spikes!

Stickers for pages 18 and 19

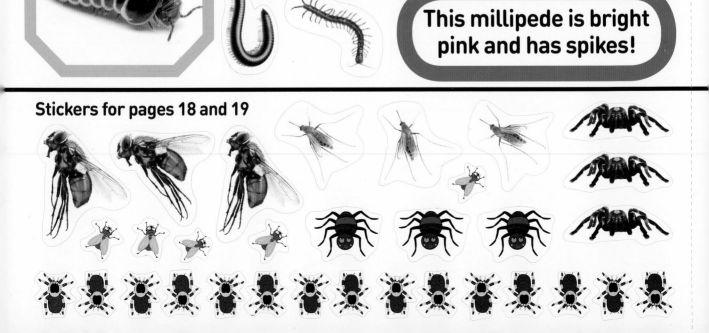

Stickers for pages 20 and 21

Stickers for pages 22 and 23

Stickers for pages 24 and 25

Extra Stickers

Stickers for pages 26 and 27

Stickers for pages 28 and 29

Stickers for pages 30 and 31

Stickers for pages 32 and 33

Stickers for pages 34 and 35

Stickers for pages 36 and 37

Stickers for pages 38 and 39

Stickers for page 40

Extra stickers

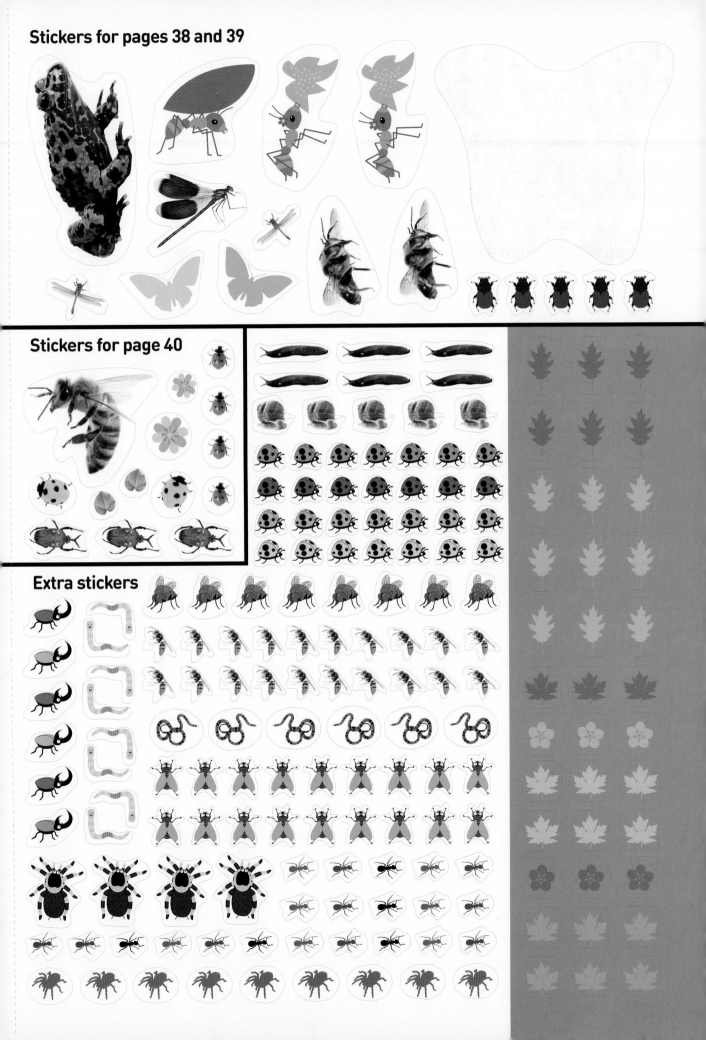

body

head

scorpion-tail spider

This spider's long body tricks other animals into thinking it is a dangerous scorpion.

golden orb spider

Help the spider through the maze to its web.

Start

Finish

All scorpions are venomous!

Young scorpions are called scorplings. They ride on their mother's back until they are old enough to live alone.

Join the dots to finish the scorpion.

Scorpions grab bugs with their claws and sting with their long tails.

Scorpions glow under UV light!

giant desert
hairy scorpion

Scorpions come out at night. Find the
stickers to throw the scorpions a dance party!

Slugs and snails are slimy!

All slugs have four "feelers" on their heads. The top two are called eye spots, while the bottom two are used for smell.

Color the slug trails to make a pattern.

garden snail

It's hard for snails to create slime, so they sometimes crawl along other snails' trails to save their energy!

banded snail

Help the snail through the maze and out of the grass.

Start

Finish

Find five hiding slugs.

Bats use sound to see in the **dark.**

Bechstein's bat

Bats screech as they fly and listen for the echoes that bounce off things around them. This helps them avoid crashing into things as they fly at night!

flying fox bat

Trace the line to help the bat fly home without crashing.

screech!

Bats don't make nests, but they find places to roost, like hollow trees, caves, and the nooks of buildings.

flying fruit bat

Start ↓

Help the bat through the maze to find its roost.

Hissing **snakes** slither and slide.

Circle the thing that doesn't belong to reveal the snake's dinner!

green tree python

Find five hiding mice.

28

eastern coral snake

Color the snake.

Burmese pythons are semiaquatic. This means they can swim as well as live on land!

Burmese python

Find all five words to finish the word search.

anaconda

boa
hunt
python
snake
swim

s	n	a	k	e	h
m	t	n	e	b	u
p	y	t	h	o	n
t	r	o	a	a	t
s	w	i	m	w	n
w	z	c	f	b	a

corn snake

29

Some snakes have venom!

Nitsche's bush vipers use their sharp fangs to inject venom into other animals.

diamondback rattlesnake

Sticker the fangs.

Sticker these really venomous snakes!

Belcher's sea snake

eastern diamondback

death adder

eastern brown snake

Inland taipan

Key:

↑ ➡ ↓ ⬅

Venomous green mambas live in trees in different parts of Africa.

Use the key to make your way through the symbol maze.

Start

Finish

Sticker a pattern on the snake.

31

Frogs live all around the world.

A poison dart frog's brightly colored body warns attackers that it is poisonous!

harlequin poison dart frog

red-headed poison dart frog

golden mantilla frog

tree frog

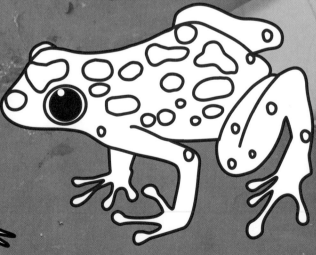

Give the frogs colorful patterns.

Join the dots to finish the frog.

Tiny glass frogs have see-through bodies!

glass frog

Pacman frog

Find the missing stickers.

33

Toads have dry, **lumpy** skin!

Fowler's toads can let out a poisonous fluid from the warts on their backs!

Woodhouse's toad

eastern American toad

Fowler's toad

Use the grid to draw the toad.

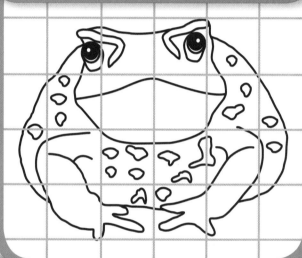

coastal plain toad

34

5 + 4 = ...

3 + 2 = ...

Colorado river toad

The fire-bellied toad shows off its red stomach to scare away any animals that might eat it.

Sticker yummy bugs for the toad to eat.

fire-bellied toad

Lizards come in lots of shapes and sizes.

The thorny devil has a "false head" on its neck. When it is scared, it ducks its real head so the false one is on show.

false head

thorny devil

green gecko

Find the missing stickers.

Gila monster

The komodo dragon is the largest lizard in the world!

Color the chameleon to match its surroundings.

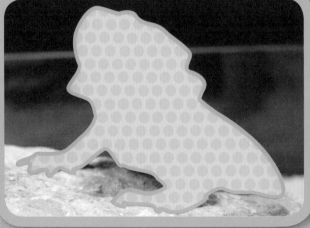

bearded dragon

A chameleon can change the color of its skin to blend in with its surroundings.

panther chameleon

Parson's chameleon

37

Explore the world of creepy-crawlies!

People who study bugs are called entomologists. Can you say the word EN-TOM-OL-OH-JIST?

Add color and stickers to finish the scene.

Search the scene. How many creatures can you count?

....

....

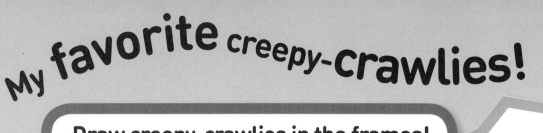

My favorite creepy-crawlies!

Draw creepy-crawlies in the frames!

coolest

weirdest

slimiest

Draw your favorite creepy-crawly.

40